A Student's Guide to

Excel 97 for Windows 95 on the PC

by

Adrian Beck

Mark Maynard

Richard Rodger

Software Made Simple
Unit E, Troon Way Business Centre,
Humberstone Lane, Leicester LE4 7JW
Telephone 0116 246 1424
Fax 0116 246 1497

Internet: http://www.s-m-s.co.uk
Email: guides@s-m-s.co.uk

THE AUTHORS

Adrian Beck is a Lecturer in Security and Information Technology at the Scarman Centre, University of Leicester

Mark Maynard is a Senior Computer Officer, Social Science Faculty, University of Leicester

Richard Rodger is a Senior Lecturer in the Economic and Social History Department, University of Leicester

OTHER GUIDES IN THIS SERIES

A Student's Guide to FileMaker Pro 2 for the Macintosh and the PC

A Student's Guide to WordPerfect 5.2 for Windows for the PC

A Student's Guide to Excel 5 for the Macintosh and the PC

A Student's Guide to Excel 4 for the Macintosh and the PC

A Student's Guide to Excel 7 for Windows 95 on the PC

A Student's Guide to Word 7 for Windows 95 on the PC

A Student's Guide to Word 97 for Windows 95 on the PC

A Student's Guide to Word 6 for Windows for the PC

A Student's Guide to Word 2 for Windows for the PC

A Student's Guide to Word 6 for the Macintosh

For further information on these guides please contact:

Software Made Simple
Unit E, Troon Way Business Centre,
Humberstone Lane, Leicester LE4 7JW
Telephone 0116 246 1424
Fax 0116 246 1497

Internet: http://www.s-m-s.co.uk
Email: guides@s-m-s.co.uk

This Guide is based on using a complete installation of Microsoft Excel 97 for Windows 95 on PC compatible with a hard disc and Windows 95. For printing use of a network is also assumed.

For simplicity the term PC is used throughout to mean IBM PC compatible.

Version 1

ISBN 1 874093 16 4

Contents

CONTENTS

Contents

1.0 INTRODUCTION

Excel's prime function is as a Spreadsheet, a powerful program for handling data, mostly numerical data. A spreadsheet is rather like an electronic accounting ledger which provides a method by which data can be analysed and used in complex calculations. It is unlikely that you will use any more than 20% of its capabilities. Consequently, this guide concentrates on those aspects of the spreadsheet which you are likely to use most.

Also covered in this guide are how to create Charts using your data and how to use Excel as a simple flat file Database.

The guide assumes a basic understanding of how to use the PC and Windows 95. If you are not confident that you have this basic understanding then read the companion guide: **A Students Guide to Word 97 for Windows 95** which contains the necessary information.

2.0 STARTING EXCEL

Microsoft
Excel

Choose **Programs** from the **Start** menu and **Microsoft Excel** from the **Programs** sub-menu or find and double-click in the icon for Excel 97.

2.1 The Office Assistant – Help Using Excel

By default Excel will probably display the **Office Assistant**. The Office Assistant is shown as an animated character in a small window and clicking once on the character will display a speech bubble into which you can type a question relating to the workings of Excel. Click on the **Search** button and the Office Assistant will try and answer your question. Usually a selection of possible answers is returned, and for further details just click on the most appropriate answer. Hide the speech bubble by clicking on the **Close** button.

Note: If for any reason the Office Assistant is not displayed, click on the 🔲 button on the Toolbar. Conversely, to hide the Office Assistant click on the **Close** 🔳 button in the Office Assistant window.

While you work the Office Assistant monitors the way you use Excel. If it has suggestions that may assist you a light bulb is displayed alongside the character and clicking on the light bulb will display the suggestion.

In addition to the Office Assistant help with any object on the screen can be obtained by choosing **What's This** from the **Help** menu and clicking on the object. More detailed help is available by choosing **Contents and Index** from the **Help** menu.

2.2

Workbooks and Worksheets

A blank workbook is displayed. A workbook is the file Excel uses to store your data.

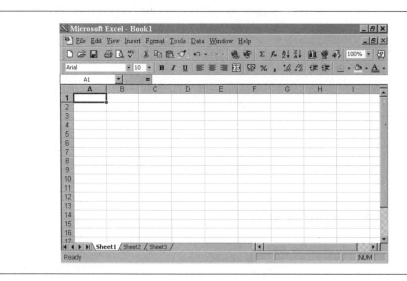

The workbook consists of worksheets (for calculating), and chart sheets (for creating charts). There are other types of sheet but these are beyond the scope of this guide. A workbook may contain a single sheet or many sheets. By default Excel opens with a workbook of 16 sheets named Sheet 1 to Sheet 16. The sheet currently in use, known as the **Active Sheet**, is indicated by the tab in bold at the bottom of the worksheet. If you wish to make a different sheet active simply click on its tab.

When you choose to save your data all the worksheets sheets are saved together as a single workbook file.

For simplicity, this guide concentrates on the use of a single worksheet which is sufficient for most needs.

2.3

Data Entry

On starting Excel a blank workbook is displayed entitled **Workbook 1**.

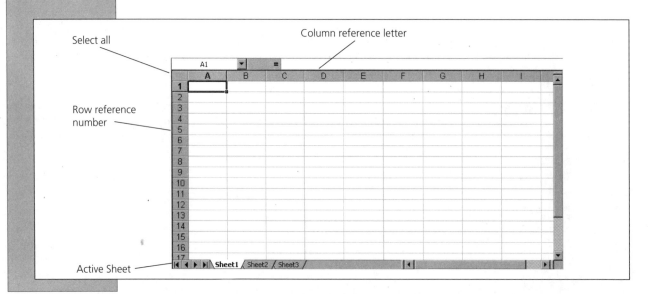

The worksheet is divided horizontally into rows and vertically into columns, as in the figure opposite. The intersection of each row and column makes a box called a **Cell** and it is into the cells that you type your data. Each cell is referenced individually by a column letter and a row number which together create a **Cell Address** or **Reference** eg. **A1**.

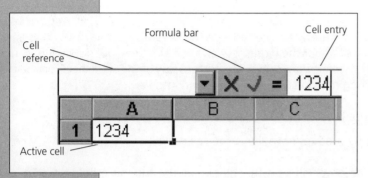

Cell reference
Formula bar
Cell entry
Active cell

To enter data in a cell move the pointer to the preferred cell and then click on the mouse button. You can type any kind of data in a cell eg. text, numbers. When you begin to type the entry it will appear in two places:

- In the cell itself, called the **Active Cell**.

- On top of the window in an area called the **Formula Bar**.

Problem? The Formula Bar is not displayed.

Solution: Select **Options** from the **Tools** menu, click on the **View** tab and click in the **Formula Bar** box.

When you have finished typing click on the in the formula bar to enter data into the worksheet. Clicking on the in the formula bar makes the active cell blank again.

Data can be entered into any cell on the worksheet. It is not necessary to start with the first cell. You can also leave cells blank if you wish.

Once data has been entered in a cell, amendments can be made by clicking on the cell and editing in the **Formula Bar**. You will find it easier to edit using the formula bar rather than editing in the cell itself.

Using the **Backspace** (←) key and clicking on the will remove the entire contents of a selected cell, or, if the pointer is in the formula bar, the **Backspace** (←) key enables you to amend the contents of the cell.

2.4 Spell Checking and AutoCorrect

To check the spelling of a Worksheet click on the button on the toolbar. If the spell checker identifies a word as spelled incorrectly a dialogue box will then be displayed listing alternative spellings. You may choose to ignore the mis-spelling. The spell checker will ignore the spelling of functions.

Excel's **AutoCorrect** feature prevents some of the most common typing errors. For example, typing two capitals together eg. EXcel, failure to capitalise days of the week, and repeated mis-types such as *teh* instead of *the* can be corrected automatically as you type when the AutoCorrect is switched on.

2.5 Moving Around the Worksheet

What you see on screen in the window is only a small part of the total worksheet. To see more of it use the scroll bars at the bottom and right hand side of the window in the same way you would for any other Windows 95 program.

2.6

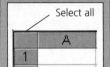

2.7

Problem? No scroll bars are shown.

Solution: Select **Options** from the **Tools** menu and click on the **Scroll Bar** boxes.

You have already seen how to move about the worksheet using the mouse. Another way is to use the **Arrow** keys which are often referred to as the **Cursor** keys. The Arrow keys enable you to move the active cell about the worksheet one cell at a time, up, down, left or right. When the active cell reaches the right side or the bottom row of the worksheet, pressing the arrow key again will bring an additional row or column into view.

The **Tab** (→|) key can be used to move the active cell to the right.

The **Enter** (↵) key can be used to move the active cell down.

Particularly useful in a large worksheet with multiple column and row entries is **Go To** in the **Edit** menu, since if you know the precise cell reference (column letter and row number), typing this will allow you to move directly to it.

The **Zoom** control box on the Toolbar can be used to take a closer look at any part of the worksheet. Just click on the arrow and drag down the required level of magnification.

Selecting Data

Often you will want to select an entire column of cells for special treatment. To do this click on the column letter. To select adjacent columns follow the above procedure and, while holding down the mouse button, drag the pointer across the columns. Similarly, several rows can be selected by clicking on their row number(s).

For columns which are not contiguous (not touching one another), select one of the columns required and then select the other by holding down the **Ctrl** key while clicking and dragging. Use the same technique to select non-contiguous rows.

Blocks of cells can be selected by clicking on the top left cell of the range and dragging diagonally to the bottom right hand cell.

To select all cells in the worksheet click on the **Select All** box. To de-select just click anywhere in the window.

To select a range of cells that extend off the screen, either click and drag from the first cell of the range to the last cell dragging past the scroll bar (the cells displayed on screen will be adjusted automatically), or alternatively, click once on the first cell of the range use the scroll bar to move to the last cell of the range and, while holding down the **Shift** (⇧) key, click once.

Types of Data

The data which you type into a worksheet is one of two types.

- **Values**: Raw data which forms the basis of the calculations.
- **Labels**: Normally text used as headings for rows and columns.

The type of data that are used for calculations are referred to as **Values**. Values can be in one of many different formats and it is important both for display and calculation purposes that the appropriate format is used. Formats are differentiated according to £ signs, number of decimal places, presence of commas dividing thousands, date formats and percentage formats.

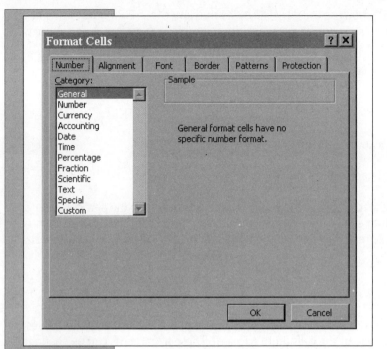

It is good practice to set the format in which you wish your data to appear before you type it. However, it is possible to amend the format subsequently.

To format values, select the cells, columns or rows which share the particular format and choose **Cell** from the **Format** menu. You will be presented with the dialogue box opposite. Click on the **Number** tab.

The format is selected choosing the category and options which correspond to your requirements.

Some examples of common number formats are shown below.

Category	Options
General	none
Number	number of decimal places, comma separator for thousands, special options for negative numbers
Currency	number of decimal places, use currency symbol (£), special options for negative numbers
Date	various date formats
Time	various time formats
Percentage	number of decimal places

If the format you want is not among the selection provided then use the **Custom** category follow the syntax and type your preferred version in the **Type** box provided.

Hint: For the most common Number formats there are buttons on the Toolbar which provide a short cut to using the menu. The 🖫 button changes the selection to Currency. The %️ button changes the selection to a Percentage. The ,️ button changes the selection to display thousands delimited by Comma. The ️ button increases the number of decimal places by one whilst the ️ button decreases the number of decimal places by one.

2.8

Changing Font, Font Style and Size

One way of changing the appearance of your selection is to change its **Font** (Typeface). As you will see by clicking on the arrow to the right of the **Font box** on the Toolbar, fonts are given all sorts of peculiar names. Select one of these fonts as you would a command from the menu bar.

E<u>xc</u>el 7

To alter the size of a selection use the down arrow to the right of the Font box. Click and drag on the arrow to the required size or type a size into the box. Sizes are measured in points or pts; 10 or 12 pts is normal, the bigger the point size the bigger the character size.

For different font styles use the buttons on the Toolbar:

B produces **bold** text.

I produces *italic* text.

U produces <u>Underlined</u> text.

To de-select any of these font styles simply select the cells and click on the particular font style button again. Other font styles are available by choosing **Cells** from the **Format** menu and from the dialogue box presented click on the **Font** tab to alter the font, font style or size as required.

Alignment

When you type in text it will be displayed on the left side of the cell (left aligned); values will be shown on the right side of the cells (right aligned). These alignments can be changed by selecting the cells to be altered, and clicking on the appropriate button on the Toolbar.

 button changes the selection to **Left Aligned**.

 button changes the selection to **Centre Aligned**.

 button changes the selection to **Right Aligned**.

Other alignments are available by choosing **Cells** from the **Format** menu and from the dialogue box presented click on the **Alignment** tab to alter the alignment as required.

To align the contents of a cell across several columns enter the data into the left hand cell, select the range of the cells across which your data is to be spread, and click on the button on the Toolbar. The gridlines between the range of selected cells will disappear indicating that a cell is centred across columns. To revert to the previous alignment select any cell in the range and click on the button on the Toolbar.

Other alignments, including the facility to rotate text in cells, are available by choosing **Cells** from the **Format** menu and from the dialogue box presented, click on the **Alignment** tab to alter the alignment as required.

Copying Formats

If you have formatted a cell or range of cells and wish to copy this format, select the cells whose format you wish to copy, click on the **Format Painter** button. Select the cell(s) you wish to copy the format to and when you release the mouse button the formats will be copied.

Note: More than one format can be copied at once using this method.

2.9

2.10

2.11 AutoFormat

Excel has built-in formats which you can apply to your data using the **AutoFormat** command. To use a built-in format select the data you wish to format and choose **AutoFormat** from the **Format** menu. The following dialogue box will be presented:

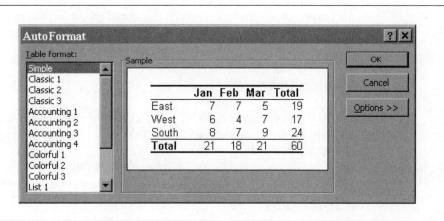

On the left is the list of built-in formats named for easy reference. In the centre is a table which displays a sample of the chosen format. Click on **OK** to apply the format to the selected range of cells.

2.12 Altering Column Widths and Row Heights

Occasionally hashes (####) appear when a column is too narrow for calculated data to be displayed in a cell. Another problem of display arises when text overflows to an adjacent cell.

Double-click here to automatically size the column

Drag to the right to make adjustments to the width of the column

To solve both these problems select the columns involved, and move the pointer to the border line that divides the column references. Notice that the pointer changes shape to ✛

Double-clicking on the border between the column reference letters when the ✛ pointer is displayed will cause the column width to be adjusted automatically to display all the cell contents of the selected columns.

To make fine adjustments to the column width, click and drag the pointer ✛. By making columns narrower more can be displayed on the screen.

The method for making rows taller or shorter is the same. Alterations to widths and heights affect complete columns or rows.

2.13 Inserting Rows, Columns and Cells

To insert a column between two existing ones, select the right hand column and choose **Columns** from the **Insert** menu. A column with the same format as that selected will be inserted. Several columns can be inserted simultaneously by selecting two, three or any number of columns and then choosing **Columns** as before. The method for inserting rows is the same.

2.14

Note: when columns and rows are inserted, all reference numbers are adjusted. Formulae references (see Section 3) are also adjusted except where cells are displaced into adjacent columns.

To insert a single cell, first select the cell where you wish it to appear, then choose **Cells** from the **Insert** menu. The dialogue box presented offers you the option of moving existing cells down or to the right. Several cells can be inserted at once by first selecting two, three or any number of cells and then choosing **Cells** as before.

Moving Data

At some stage you will want to move a block of data from one place in the worksheet to another. Excel provides you with two techniques for doing this and so avoiding the trouble and errors involved in retyping:

- Drag and Drop
- Cut, Copy and Paste

Drag and Drop

Drag and Drop is most useful for moving a small number of cells for short distances about a worksheet.

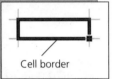
Cell border

- Select the cells that you wish to move and release the mouse button.

- Move the pointer to the border of the selection and when it changes shape from the cross to an arrow, click and drag the selection to its new position. If the new position of the text is currently not on screen, you can cause the text to scroll by moving the pointer to the top or bottom of the screen.

To copy a piece of text leaving the original intact hold down the **Ctrl** key while dragging. Note that a **+** sign is shown alongside the pointer.

If you wish to insert the selection between other data hold down the **Shift** (⇑) key before releasing the mouse button. Note that for guidance the pointer is followed by a shaded rectangle.

Problem? Drag and Drop does not appear to work.

Solution: Choose **Options** from the **Tools** menu and from the dialogue box presented click on the **Edit** tab and click on the **Allow Cell Drag and Drop** box.

Note that the reference of the cell or cells being dragged is indicated in a pop-up box alongside the selection.

Cut, Copy and Paste

It is best to use Cut, Copy and Paste when moving large numbers of cells of data and transferring data between programs.

To move cells of data deleting the original:

- Select the cells to be moved.

- Choose **Cut** from the **Edit** menu. Click on the cell at the top left hand corner of its new position and choose **Paste** from the **Edit** menu.

Hint: A short cut to using the cut, copy and paste commands is to use the buttons on the Toolbar: the ✂ button Cuts, the 📋 button Copies and the 📋 button Pastes.

To move a piece of data leaving the original in place, repeat the above using **Copy** from the **Edit** menu instead of **Cut**. Note that a dotted line appears around the copied data.

For information on copying and pasting formulae see Section 3.4. For more information about copying and pasting data between programs see Appendix C.

Deleting Data

2.15

Any deletion should be performed with care, especially if you are deleting entire rows or columns. You may choose to delete cells including their contents or just the contents itself.

To delete cells and their contents: select the cells you wish to remove and choose **Delete** from the **Edit** menu. From the dialogue box presented choose whether to move the remaining cells up or to the left.

To delete just the contents of cells: select the cells whose contents you want to remove. Next, choose **Clear** from the **Edit** menu, and **Contents** from the sub-menu.

Undo

2.16

One useful facility you will soon grow to love is **Undo**. This is available by clicking on the button on the toolbar. Clicking on the down arrow to the right of the button lists the last changes made and these can be undone by choosing the appropriate item on the list.

Conversely, using the **Redo** button on the toolbar reverses any changes you have made using the Undo button.

Creating a Series Using AutoComplete

2.17

Two common requirements when entering data are the repetition of a particular number across a range of cells and the creation of a series. There are many different types of series, and some examples are shown below.

Date and Time related:

  9:00, 10:00, 11:00, 12:00

  Mon, Tue, Wed, Thur

  Monday, Tuesday, Wednesday, Thursday

  Apr, Mar, Feb, Jan

  1st Jan, 2nd Jan, 3rd Jan, 4th Jan

  1986, 1988, 1990, 1992

  1860, 1861, 1862, 1863

Linear related:

  1, 2, 3, 4

  1, 3, 5, 7

  200, 150, 100, 50

The technique used for creating a series is called **AutoComplete**.

- At the start of the range of cells enter two examples of the series into two contiguous cells.

- Select the two cells and drag the handle which appears in the bottom right hand corner of the selection across the required range. When you release the mouse button the series will be displayed in the cells that you have dragged across. Note that as you drag across the required range a pop-up box indicates the last value in the range.

Repeating a Number Across a Range of Cells

- At the start of the range of cells enter the number you wish to repeat.

- Select the cell and drag the handle which appears in the bottom right hand corner across the required range. When you release the mouse button the contents of the cell will be repeated in the cells that you have dragged across.

CALCULATING

Formulae are at the heart of the spreadsheet. They are what make the spreadsheet special since they enable rapid arithmetical or statistical calculations to be made. They can be written quickly and easily to perform calculations such as averages, percentages and totals on the entire range of data, or part of it, as well as many more complex routines (see Appendix B).

Simple Formulae

It is essential to remember that the formula is written into a cell where the result of the calculation is required. The result is shown in the cell when the ✔ on the formula bar is clicked, or when the insertion point is moved to another cell.

The formula is a set of instructions to the computer. It has four elements:

SUM	▼	X ✔ =	=A1+A2
	A	**B**	**C**
1	1		
2	2		
3	=A1+A2		

- The **=** symbol that must be used to start a formula. This lets Excel know that what you type next is a calculation.

- The references of **cells** on which you wish to perform a calculation.

- **Mathematical operators**: +,-,*(multiply) and / (divide). You can also use brackets in your calculation.

- **Functions**: Use of functions in a formula is optional. Some functions have arguments, including cell references, associated with them. All these must be enclosed in brackets. For a list of the most useful functions see Appendix B.

The simplest of formulae do not use functions. Here are some examples:

=A1+A2	This adds.cells A1 and A2 together.
=A1*B1	This multiplies cells A1 and B1.
=A1/A2+(A3+A4)	This divides A1 by A2 and adds A3 and A4 to the result.

Functions

If you have many cells you wish to add or multiply together, or on which you wish to perform some statistical operation, it would be laborious to have to type each cell reference in as in the simple formula:

=A2+B2+C2+D2+E2+F2...etc.

You might also introduce errors in the formula. Using **Functions** offers an important shortcut. Understanding functions will enable you to automate many procedures and manipulate your data to greater effect. Indeed without them, your use of Excel will be severely curtailed.

3.0

3.1

3.2

Here are some examples of Formulae that use functions:

=SUM(A1:D1) This sums the contents of cells A1, B1, C1 and D1. The presence of the colon indicates that all cells between those referenced are to be used by the formula.

=AVERAGE(A1:A4) This averages, or provides the mean of, the contents of cells A1, A2, A3 and A4.

=STDEV(A1:A4) This finds standard deviation of cells A1, A2, A3 and A4.

Cell references etc. entered into the parenthesis are called arguments. For a list of the most useful functions see Appendix B.

How to Use Formulae and Functions

3.3

- Select the cell in which you wish the result of the calculation to appear. Usually this is at the bottom of a column of cells or to the right of a row of cells which form the basis of the calculation. However, it could be anywhere on the worksheet except in a cell that will be referred to in the calculation.

- Click on the = in the Formula Bar and the **Formula Palette** will appear.

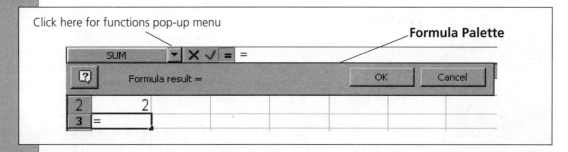

Click here for functions pop-up menu

Formula Palette

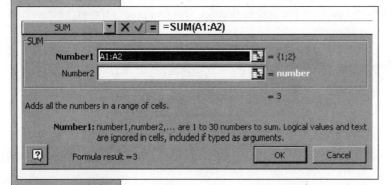

- If a **Function** is to be used choose the required function from the (functions) pop-up menu on the Formula Bar. The Formula Palette is then expanded to include a description of the function and allows 'arguments' required by the function to be entered.

- Arguments can consist of cell references and any relationships that apply to them. If required, you can use mathematical operators between the references. In many cases Excel will automatically enter the cell references for you. However, if you wish to manually specify a range of cells that are contiguous (touching one another) it is only necessary to type in the first and last cell references, separated by a colon. For quick entry in a cell range click on the first cell of the range and while holding down the mouse button drag to the last cell of the range. The cell references and colon will be entered automatically for you. If you wish to calculate using cells that are not contiguous, just type in their references separated by commas.

Note: To view cells beneath the Formula Palette click and drag it to a new location. Alternatively, hide the Formula Palette by clicking on the ▣ button on the Palette. To display it once again click on the ▣ button.

- Click on the **OK** button to perform the calculation and the result of the calculation will be shown in the cell where the formula was typed. If for any reason Excel interprets the formula to be incorrect you will be alerted (see Error Messages in Appendix A).

- To amend any formula just click in the cell containing the formula and edit in the Formula Bar. Checking the range of cells referenced by a function can be assisted by selecting the cell containing the function and moving the insertion point into the Formula Bar; the references are highlighted in blue.

- You are not limited to using a single function within a formula, formulae can be as complex as required. To add further functions to a formula click in the cell containing the formula, and within the Formula Bar move the insertion point to where you wish to add the further function and add the function as above.

A short cut is to make use of the **SUM** function by clicking on the Σ button on the Toolbar. This will guess at the range of cell references that you wish to sum and insert them into the function for you. Edit the formula if this does not coincide exactly with the range of cells you do in fact want to use.

Calculating Using Text Labels

Lets face it, most people could relate better to the formula 'Profit = Price Sold - Price Bought' than they could 'C2=A2-B2' ! This is where using text labels in formulae comes in. Text labels let you use words instead of cell references to describe what you wish calculated – for example the Profit formula above would be perfectly valid.

To use text labels in a formula requires you to have provided labels or headings for the columns or rows you wish to use in your calculation – in our example the column labels would be Price Sold and Price Bought. In the cell where you wish the calculation to appear simply enter these labels into the calculation and click on the ☑ as normal. Our example is shown below:

C2	▼	=	=Price Sold - Price Bought	
	A	B	C	D
1	Price Sold	Price Bought	Profit	
2	150	100	50	

In addition labels can be used to help calculate with columns or rows. For example, to calculate the total profit the formula below can be used:

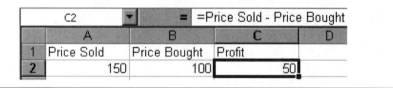

C5	▼	=	=SUM(Profit)
	A	B	C
1	Price Sold	Price Bought	Profit
2	150	100	50
3	125	110	15
4	150	130	20
5			85

AutoComplete (see Section 3.4) can be used to extend the formula to other cells.

IMPORTANT: By default formulae which use labels reference their cells absolutely. This is in contrast to formulae using cell references that are by default relatively referenced. See Section 3.5 to learn about absolute and relative cell references.

3.4

Copying Formulae Using AutoComplete

Typing in the odd formula is all very well, but if you have a worksheet that performs the same calculation on column upon column of cells it can be tedious to type the same formula over and over again, the only difference being the range of cells referenced.

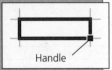

Handle

There is an easier way, by applying an existing formula. Select the cell with the formula which you wish to apply to another group of cells. Click and drag the handle across the range of cells to which you wish the formula to apply and release the mouse button. This will copy the formula and apply it **relative** to the new range of cells on the worksheet. So the formula =SUM(B2:B3) typed into cell B4 and clicked and dragged into cell E4 will now look like =SUM(E2:E3).

B4	▼	=	=SUM(B2:B3)

	A	B	C	D	E
1		1989	1990	1991	1992
2	Electricity	12	15	18	22
3	Gas	6	8	15	17
4	Total	18			

E4	▼	=	=SUM(E2:E3)

	A	B	C	D	E
1		1989	1990	1991	1992
2	Electricity	12	15	18	22
3	Gas	6	8	15	17
4	Total	18	23	33	39

Click and drag on the handle from cell B4 to cell E4 to copy the formula in cell B4 to the other cells.

To copy the formula into a range of cells which are not adjacent to the cell containing the formula, select the cell containing the formula and while holding down the **Ctrl** key, click and drag its border to copy the cell to the first cell of the range. As above click and drag the handle across the range of cells to which you want the formula to apply.

Although these examples of formulae have all applied to calculations involving columns of data, with results appearing below the data you can also perform calculations on rows where the result appears to the right of the data. These formulae can be clicked and dragged in just the same way.

3.5

Absolute and Relative References

Up to this point all formulae references have been **Relative**. That is, if a formula is moved the cells to which it refers are changed according to its new position on the worksheet. We have seen how useful this can be when **Copying** and **Pasting** formulae.

Occasionally, it is useful to have a formula reference the same cells no matter where on the worksheet the formula is moved. For example, you might always want to refer to a constant value that you have typed into a particular cell on the worksheet. This is called an **Absolute** reference. Where some of the cells to which the formula refers are absolute, type a **$** symbol before both the row number and column letter. So a relative cell reference of A1 becomes A1. Occasionally, you may wish the rows to be relative but the columns to be absolute. To do this put a **$** symbol in front of the column reference only, eg. $A1.

The example below multiplies the total by the constant 'Tax' in cell B7. Note that when the formula is clicked and dragged the cell reference B7 remains constant due to the presence of the **$** symbols.

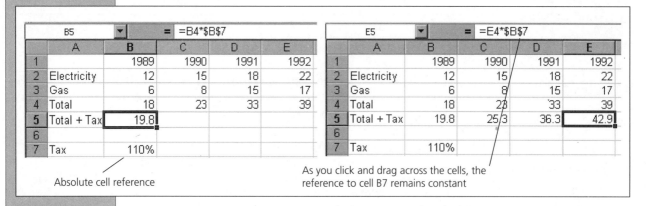

Absolute cell reference

As you click and drag across the cells, the reference to cell B7 remains constant

Note: a quick way to change a relative reference into an absolute reference in the formula bar is to select the cell references you wish to change and then press the **F4** key. The $ symbol is added to both the column and row references. Press the **F4** key again to make only the row references absolute, and again to make only the column references absolute.

3.6 Goal-Seeking

Goal-Seeking is useful if you know the result you want from a formula but you don't know a particular value the formula needs to achieve the result.

	A	B	C
	B5	▼ = =AVERAGE(B1:B3)	
1	Theory course work	51	
2	Experimental course work	55	
3	Examination		
4			
5	Final Result	53	

In the example opposite:

The pass mark for the course overall is an average of 60% and the student wishes to calculate the Examination mark she needs to attain taking into account her course work marks.

To calculate the examination mark required, ensure that the cell displaying the **Final Result** contains the calculation to average the three marks and choose **Goal Seek** from the **Tools** menu.

In the dialogue box presented, first enter the cell reference of the Final Result into the **Set cell** box, and then enter the value you wish the result to goal seek in the box alongside **To value**. In our case this is 60. In the box alongside **By changing cell**, click on cell B3 to enter the reference of the cell you wish to change. Click on **OK** and the required value will be calculated.

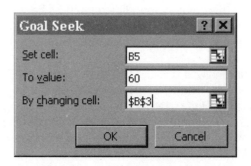

4.0

MANAGING A WORKSHEET

Excel has a number of features which enable you both to accelerate and to manage your worksheet more efficiently.

4.1

Borders and Shading

You can highlight a selected cell or group of cells with a border by clicking on the arrow alongside the ▢▾ button on the toolbar and choosing the border you require from those displayed.

To alter the fill colour of a selection click on the arrow alongside the ◇▾ button on the toolbar and choose the required colour.

To alter the font colour of a selection click on the arrow alongside the A▾ button on the toolbar and choose the required colour.

4.2

Automatic and Manual Recalculation

When you alter data in cells which are used in a calculation Excel normally updates calculations automatically. Indeed this is a powerful feature of the spreadsheet. However, if you have a very large worksheet with many inter-dependent calculations this updating can be slow. To circumvent this Excel allows you to turn off the default **Automatic** re-calculation and instead opt for **Manual**. To do this choose **Options** from the **Tools** menu and from the dialogue box presented click first on the **Calculation** tab and then on the **Manual** button.

Now a re-calculation is performed only when you press the **Ctrl** and **=** keys or **F9**.

Note: Ensure that the formula bar is not active when manually re-calculating.

4.3

Freezing Panes

Occasionally, you might have column or row headings which you would like to remain stationary while the remainder of the worksheet scrolled normally. First you need to split the window. Do this by clicking and dragging the small rectangle at the top (for a row) or right (for a column) of the scroll bar. Drag until it exposes the row or column that you want to freeze. You can now scroll either part of the split window independently. Choose **Freeze Panes** from the **Window** menu to freeze the upper or right pane.

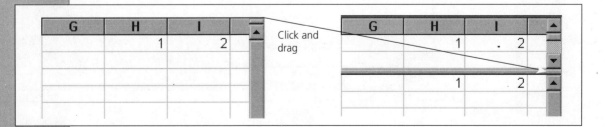

Click and drag

4.4

Display Options

You can choose to display gridlines, formulae, row and column headings (reference numbers and letters), page breaks etc. Choose **Options** from the **Tools** menu, and from the dialogue box presented click on the **View** tab and choose your display preferences.

Note: What is displayed on screen is not necessarily the same as what is printed. There are options here that can be confused with options in **Page Setup** dialogue box. Only the Formulas option will be printed.

4.5

Comments

It is sometimes useful to be able to attach some text to a cell eg. you might want to include the source of a particular piece of data. You can do this by using the **Comment** command. Select the cell to which your text relates, choose **Comment** from the **Insert** menu, and type your text into the box provided. Text will wrap on to the next line of the box, as with wordprocessing, so you don't need to press the **Enter** (↵) key at the end of each line. Click on any other cell when you have finished.

Notice that a small red triangle appears in the top right corner of the cell. When the pointer passes over a cell containing a Comment the text contained in the cell is displayed.

Text in a Comment can be edited by selecting the cell and choosing **Edit Comment** from the **Insert** menu. Edit as you would using a wordprocessor.

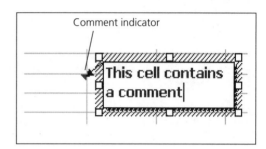

Comment indicator

This cell contains a comment

5.0

SAVING, OPENING AND EXITING

5.1

Saving Your Workbook

When you decide that you wish to stop using Excel you should save your workbook so that you can continue another day. To save a newly created workbook choose **Save As** from the **File** menu. A dialogue box appears like the one below.

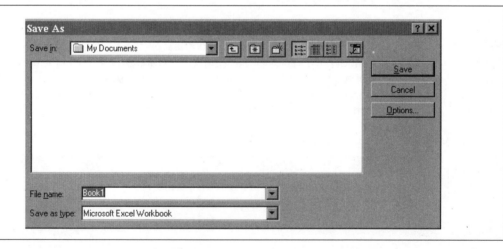

By default workbooks are usually saved to a folder called 'My Documents' on the hard disc or network disc. If you wish to save to a different disc click on the down arrow alongside the **Save In** box and choose the disc from those listed. If you wish to save to a different folder double-click on the folder from those listed in the dialogue box.

Next replace the default file name '**Book1**' in the file name box with an appropriate file name for your workbook.

To save your workbook either click on the **Save** button or press the **Enter** (↵) key. The workbook has now been saved as a file on the disc you specified.

> **Note**: When a Workbook is saved all sheets – Worksheets and Chart sheets are saved together.

A titled file (one that has been saved previously) can be updated and replaced by using the **Save** command from the **File** menu or by clicking on the **Save** button 🖫 on the Toolbar.

If you wish to create a folder into which to save your workbook click on the 📁 button from the **Save** dialogue box, enter a name for the folder and double-click on the newly created folder from the dialogue box. Clicking on **Save** will save your workbook into this folder.

Opening a Workbook

5.2

Choose **Open** from the **File** menu or click on the 📂 button on the Toolbar. A dialogue box appears (similar to the Save dialogue box shown previously), and this lists all the files or workbooks which can be opened by Excel. To open a particular file select the disc by clicking on the arrow alongside the **Look in** box and choose the disc from those listed. If the file was saved into a particular folder double-click on the folder from those listed in the dialogue box. When the desired file name appears in the dialogue box, open it in one of two ways: either by clicking on the file name and then on the **Open** button, or by double-clicking the file name.

> **Hint**: A short-cut to opening one of four most recently used workbooks is to choose the name of the workbook from those listed at the bottom of the **File** menu.

If the Excel program itself is not yet open existing workbooks can also be opened by locating their icon and double-clicking.

To open a new workbook choose **New** from the **File** menu, or as a shortcut, click on 📄 the button on the Toolbar.

Closing a Workbook and Exiting

5.3

To stop working on your workbook choose **Close** from the **File** menu. If you have not saved or have made any changes you will be asked if you wish to save the workbook. **Yes** saves all changes before closing or exiting; **No** closes the file without saving any changes since the last save. The **Cancel** button cancels the **Close** or **Exit** command.

To conclude using Excel altogether simply choose **Exit** from the **File** menu.

PRINTING

6.0

You may have noticed an option under the File menu called Print. **DON'T** use this just yet. First you must check that your workbook is set up correctly.

The Page Setup

6.1

Choose the command **Page Setup** from the **File** menu. This presents a dialogue box like the one over.

Along the top of the dialogue box is a series of Tabs. Clicking on one of these tabs displays options relating to the tab title. Click on the **Page** tab and check that the paper set up is for A4 and that the orientation is correct.

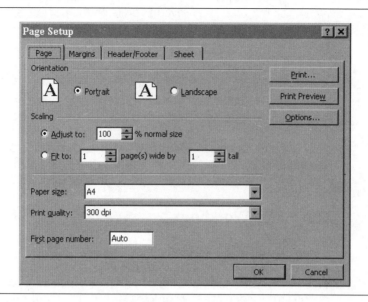

You can also adjust the position on the page on which the worksheet is printed by changing the size of the margins. To print the worksheet in the centre of the page click on the **Margins** tab and on the **Centre Horizontally** and **Vertically** boxes.

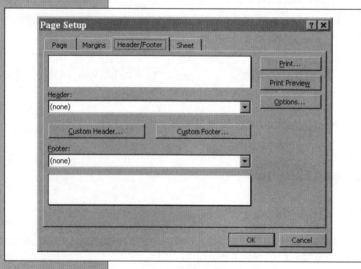

By default Excel prints a header at the top of each printed page consisting of the name of the file. To remove this and insert your own header click on the **Header/Footer** tab and on the **Custom Header** button. The header is divided into three sections representing text inserted to the left, centre, and right of the top of the page. To insert text so that it appears at the top centre of each page of the workbook delete any characters in the centre section and insert your text.

Likewise, by clicking on the **Custom Footer** button the default footer consisting of the word '**Page**' and the page number can be deleted or amended if required.

You may also wish to have a particular column or row printed out on every page – this can be particularly useful for headings. To do this click on the **Sheet** tab and enter the row number alongside **Rows to Repeat at Top**. Similarly, for columns enter the column letter alongside **Columns to Repeat at Left**.

Selecting What to Print

The next step is to specify exactly which cells are to be printed, and between which cells you wish the page breaks to occur. Of course, if you wish to print the whole of the worksheet and it doesn't occupy more than a page you can disregard this. Otherwise you need to follow the instructions below.

- First to select the area of cells you wish to print, choose **Print Area** from the **File** menu and **Set Print Area** from the sub-menu. Omit this step if you wish to print the entire worksheet.

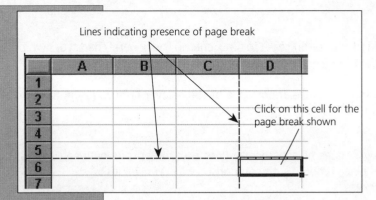

Lines indicating presence of page break

Click on this cell for the page break shown

• Next, you must specify where on the worksheet the page breaks are to appear. Excel automatically fits as many cells as possible on to a page, and puts a dotted line on the cell border where a page break occurs. However, this may not be where you want the page break. Define your own page break by clicking on the cell above and to the left of where you wish the page break to appear (see opposite). Then choose **Page Break** from the **Insert** menu.

To check the position of page breaks choose **Page Break Preview** from the **View** menu. Page breaks and their respective page numbers are displayed in a magnified view.

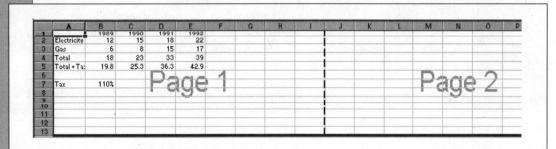

• Lastly choose **Print Preview** from the **File** menu and you will be shown a 'bird's eye view' of how the worksheet will appear when printed. This is useful since you can check all your print settings. To take a closer look click on the **Zoom** button and use the scroll bars to move about the worksheet. The **Next** and **Previous** buttons show the adjacent pages of the worksheet. If what appears on screen is not exactly as you want printed, click on the **Close** button to return to the worksheet.

Note: If you are unable to fit all the data you wish to on to a page either, adjust the width of the columns to accommodate more data on to a page (see Section 2.10) or adjust the scaling of the page from the **Page** tab on the **Page Setup** dialogue box.

6.3 Printing

Choose **Print** from the **File** menu.

If you wish to print only a selection of pages enter the page numbers into the appropriate boxes.

After you have made your final print choices click on the **OK** button.

Hint: As a short cut to printing, if you have chosen the printer set up you wish to use just click on the 🖶 button on the Toolbar.

Problem? Gridlines and/or row and column headings are printed even though these are not displayed on the worksheet.

Solution: Choose **Page Setup** from the **File** menu, click on the **Sheet** tab, click in the **Gridlines** and/or **Row and Column Headings** boxes as required and then on **OK**.

7.0

CHARTS

Excel uses data contained in the worksheet to draw charts. The general chart types which are available are shown below as are definitions for the terms used.

 Area
Displays the relative importance of values over time with emphasis on the amount of change.

 Bar
Displays values at a particular time or comparisons between values. Bar charts place emphasis on comparison between values.

 Column
Displays values over time or comparisons between values. Column charts place emphasis on comparison between values.

 Line
Displays trends in data over time at **regular** intervals with emphasis on time and rate of change. For data series sampled at irregular intervals an XY (Scatter) chart is more suitable.

 Pie
Displays the relationship between the value and the whole as a proportion. Only suitable for displaying the relationships of one data set at a time.

 Doughnut
As Pie chart but can display relationships between more than one data series at a time.

 Radar
Displays variations in data series relative to a central point and between one another.

 XY (Scatter)
Displays the relationship between values of several data sets as points on the chart. Useful if data series over time are at **irregular** intervals. Points for particular data sets can be joined with lines if required.

 Surface
The best combinations between two sets of data.

 Bubble
A variation of the XY (scatter) chart where the size of the marker shows the value of a further variable.

 Stock
Sometimes termed a Hi-Lo chart it illustrates a band through which a variable moves.

 **Cone, Cylinder, Pyramid** Alternative shapes to the standard 3D column and bar charts. Once created each type of chart can be refined to suit your needs.

Terms defined:

Throughout this guide and while using Excel several terms are used that require clarification. The terms are defined here where relevant with reference to the fictitious data below.

Data series →

Category →

	1989	1990	1991	1992
Electricity	12	15	18	22
Gas	6	8	15	17

→ Values

Category – Category data is usually plotted on the X (horizontal) axis of a chart. Exceptions 3D charts, XY (Scatter) charts, Bar charts.

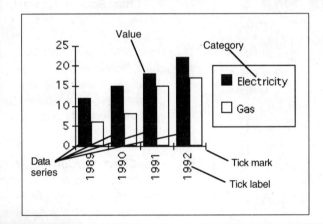

Value – Values are usually plotted on the Y (vertical) axis of a chart. Exceptions 3D charts, XY (Scatter) charts, Bar charts.

Data series – A series of data plotted on the chart eg. the cost of Electricity for the years 1989,1990,1991,1992.

Tick marks – A small line on the axis that divides categories, the scale or a data series.

Tick labels – Text associated with tick marks.

7.1 Selecting Data for a Chart

You must first select the data which will form the basis of the chart. Data may be either in rows or columns and any number of each may be selected.

Contiguous columns/rows (columns/rows which are touching) can easily be selected by clicking and dragging across the range of cells. Select the cells NOT the row numbers or column letters.

	A	B	C	D	E
1		1989	1990	1991	1992
2	Electricity	12	15	18	22
3	Gas	6	8	15	17

To select columns that are not contiguous, select one of the columns as above, and then select other columns by holding down the **Ctrl** key while clicking and dragging. Use the same technique to select non-contiguous rows.

7.2 Creating the Chart

A chart can be created in two ways: embedded in the worksheet along with any data or on its own in a chart sheet as part of a workbook. Creating an embedded chart has the advantage that it can be easily viewed and printed along with data in the worksheet. Creating a chart sheet has the advantage that it can be viewed and printed independent of the worksheet from which it was derived. In both cases the chart and the data will be saved together in the workbook.

The easiest way to create a chart is to use the **Chart Wizard**.

To create a chart select the data to be used and click on the  **Chart Wizard** button on the Toolbar. A series of chart wizard dialogue boxes are displayed.

7.3 The Chart Wizard

Follow the instructions in the four dialogue boxes displayed. Click on the **Next** button of each dialogue box to proceed.

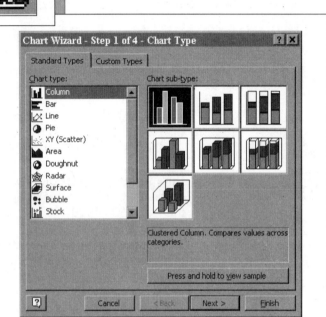

① This **Chart Type** dialogue box requires you to choose the standard chart type, eg. line, column etc. The chart type can be further refined by clicking on the **Custom Types** tab.

② This **Chart Source Data** dialogue box merely asks for confirmation of the range of cells which contains the data from which you wish to create the chart. You can also choose whether the data should be displayed as columns or rows. A sample chart using your selected data is displayed in the dialogue box.

③ This **Chart Options** dialogue box provides tabbed options relating to chart titles, axes, gridlines, legend, data labels and the data table.

Note: Chart options are explained in detail in subsequent sections.

④ This **Chart Location** dialogue box allows you to choose whether to create the chart embedded on the worksheet or in a separate chart sheet.

The chart is drawn to your specifications when the **Finish** button is clicked in the fourth dialogue box.

7.4 Chart Data Options

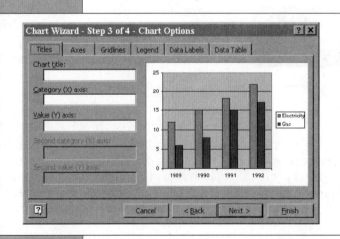

The format of your data influences the way Excel creates charts. You may prefer a different appearance, and so the third dialogue box of the Chart Wizard provides options for a different presentation of the chart. Not all the options are available for every type of chart. The most common options are listed here.

• Click on Rows or Columns depending on which you wish to be displayed as data series on the chart.

- The contents of the first rows/columns specified will be displayed as labels along the X axis.

- The contents of the first rows/columns specified will be displayed as the legend text.

- The contents of the first rows/columns specified will be displayed pie slice labels.

- The contents of the first rows/columns specified will be displayed as the chart title.

7.5 Moving and Resizing an Embedded Chart

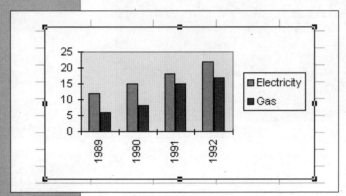

Charts can be moved around the worksheet by clicking and dragging the centre of the chart.

To resize a chart: click once on the chart – this will put handles in the corners and along each side of the chart.

The handles can then be clicked and dragged to make the chart bigger, smaller, taller or wider.

Note: It may be necessary for you to alter the font size of any text in a resized chart as text is sized independently of the chart.

8.0 FORMATTING A CHART

Though Excel will format your chart automatically, occasionally this format will not be acceptable and the chart will need customising.

8.1 Changing the Chart Type

Select the chart and choose **Chart Type** from the **Chart** menu and then the preferred chart type from those displayed.

The chart type of a data series can be altered independently of other series in the chart. Just select the series and choose the chart type as above.

Problem? There is no **Chart** menu.

Solution: Select the chart and try again!

8.2 Changing the Fill Pattern or Colour of an Area

The fill pattern and colour of areas in pie slices, bars, columns, plot area, and their backgrounds can be altered.

To do so double-click on the area to be filled, eg. bar of a bar chart, plot area, chart area etc. This will display a dialogue box from which you can choose the required colours and patterns.

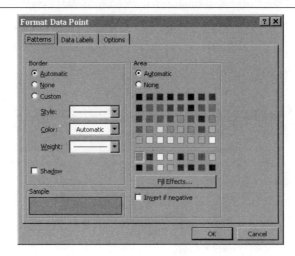

8.3 Adding a Legend

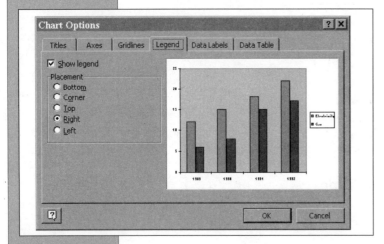

Adding a legend to a chart clearly differentiates one plotted variable from another. Using shaded areas or plot symbols emphasises the distinctions between the variables.

To add a legend to your chart choose **Chart Options** from the **Chart** menu and click on the **Legend** tab. Check the **Show Legend** box and choose the default placement of the legend. Click on **OK** to add the legend to the chart.

The legend can repositioned and resized by clicking and dragging as outlined in Section 7.5.

To alter the font or border of the legend double-click on it and make the necessary changes from the dialogue box displayed.

8.4 Adding Text to a Chart

To add text to a chart enter the text into the formula bar and click on the ☑ mark. The text will be displayed on the chart surrounded by handles. Click and drag on the text to reposition it, and on the handles to resize it. See Section 7.5 for more information about handles.

8.5 Formatting and Deleting Text

The appearance or format of any chart text can be altered in a variety of ways: font and font style can be changed, orientation of text changed to vertical or rotated, colour and pattern of text and text background changed.

To change the formatting of any chart text double-click on the text you wish to change. From the dialogue box displayed choose the tab appropriate to the formatting you wish to change, make the necessary changes, and click on the **OK** button.

To delete text, select the border around the text and press the **Backspace** (←) key.

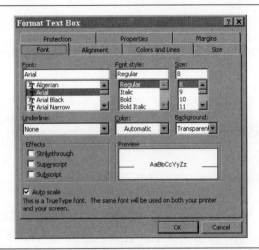

8.6 Using Arrows in a Chart

Sometimes it can be useful to highlight a particular aspect of your chart with an arrow. To add an arrow:

- Click on the [button] button on the Toolbar and the Drawing Toolbar is displayed.

- Click on the [button] button on this Toolbar.

- To move the arrow click and drag its start and end points.

- To change the orientation, click and drag one of the handles at either end of the arrow.

- To add text to the arrow see Section 8.4.

To delete an arrow, select it, and press the Backspace (←) key.

To format an arrow double-click on it. A dialogue box will be presented which allows you to choose your preferred format from a range of options.

8.7 Gridlines

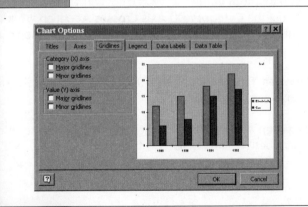

If you have a large chart it can be particularly useful to add gridlines to assist in comparing variables. To add either major or minor gridlines:

Choose **Chart Options** from the **Chart** menu.

From the dialogue box displayed choose the **Gridlines** tab, click on the check boxes of the gridlines you require and click on the **OK** button.

To alter the style and weight (thickness) of the gridlines double-click on the gridline, and from the dialogue box presented select the format you prefer.

8.8 Axes

By default all axes are shown on the chart. If you do not want to display a particular axis choose **Chart Options** from the **Chart** menu, click on the **Axes** tab, and un-check on the required check box(es).

To alter the appearance of the axis, tick marks, axis labels and scale just double-click on the axis concerned. From the dialogue box presented click on the appropriate tab and make the required changes. Options available from the **Scale** tab require further explanation (see below).

8.9 Altering the Scale of an Axis

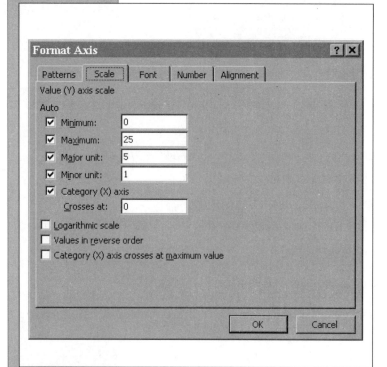

The following options are available from the **Scale** tab though not all are available with every chart or axis type:

Minimum/Maximum - Defines the smallest/largest data value to be displayed.

Major/Minor Unit - Defines the increment between major/minor tick marks.

Category (X) Axis Crosses At - Moves the position of the X axis to the value you specify. With Scatter charts this option changes to **Value (Y) Crosses At**. With 3D charts this option changes to **Floor (XY Plane) Crosses At**.

Values In Reverse Order - Inverts the chart scale eg. lowest scale at the top highest at the bottom.

Logarithmic Scale - Converts the linear scale into a logarithmic scale.

Category (X) Axis Crosses At Maximum Value - Moves the position of the X axis to after the highest value. This option overrides the **Category (X) Axis Crosses At** option. With a Scatter Chart this option changes to **Value (Y) axis Crosses At**. With a 3D chart this option changes to **Floor (XY) Plane Crosses At**.

Number Of Categories Between Tick Mark Labels - Defines how many categories that you wish to label, eg. 2 will label every other category.

Number Of Categories Between Tick Marks - Defines where you wish to display tick marks, eg. 2 will put a tick mark between every other category.

8.10 Formatting Data Series

The patterns, axis, name and values, Y error bars, X values and data labels can also be altered for each series. To make such changes double-click on one of the values in the series. The **Format Data Series** dialogue box will be displayed with various options appropriate to the type of chart concerned.

The chart type of a particular data series can be altered independently of other series in the chart. See Section 8.1.

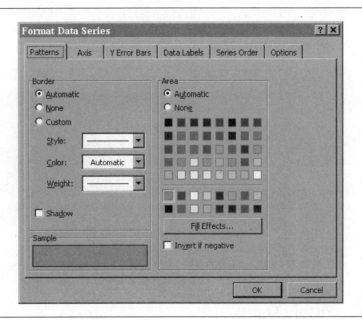

8.11 Adding New Data to a Chart

If data used to create the chart is changed then this is automatically reflected in the chart. Axes are altered accordingly.

If you wish to add a new data series:

- Ensure that the chart is selected.

- Choose **Add Data** from the **Chart** menu. This displays the **Add Data** dialogue box.

- With the dialogue box on screen select the range of cells containing the data you wish to add to your chart. If necessary you can move the dialogue box. The references for these cells will be displayed in the dialogue box.

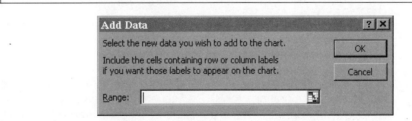

- Click on **OK** and the data will be added to the chart.

8.12 Deleting a Chart

To delete an embedded chart, first select it, then choose **Clear** from the **Edit** menu and **All** from the sub-menu.

To delete a chart sheet containing the chart, choose **Delete Sheet** from the **Edit** menu.

8.13 Special 3D Chart Options

When you plot a 3D chart **3D View** is available from the **Chart** menu. On choosing this command the following dialogue box is presented which allows you to specify the angle of elevation, angle of rotation and perspective of the chart. A sample view of a 3D chart displays the effect of your actions.

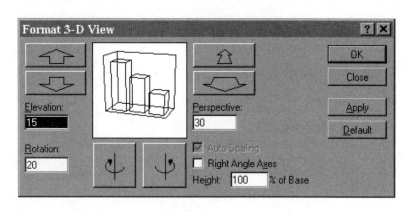

8.14 Picture Charts

Bar, Column and Line charts can be modified to include pictures as data series markers as in the charts shown below:

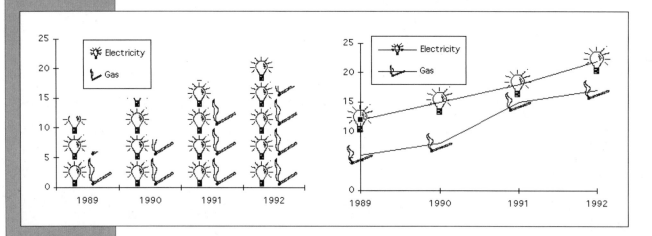

To use pictures in this way you need first to have created the graphic. Graphics are best drawn by using a graphics program but the graphics facility in Excel can be used. Click on 🔲 to get access to the graphics tools. See Section 10 for more about Excel's graphing facilities. Either way, for best results it is advisable to keep the graphic as simple as possible.

- Create your graphic.

- Select the graphic and choose **Copy** from the **Edit** menu.

- If you are using a graphics program **Exit** the program and **Open** Excel.

- Select the chart and select the data series with the marker you wish to replace by the picture.

- Choose **Paste** from the **Edit** menu. The graphic will replace the chosen column or marker.

- If the graphic is pasted to a column you can specify whether the graphic is stretched or stacked to make up the length of the column and whether the graphic is scaled. To do this double-click on the data series, click on the **Patterns** tab and on the **Fill Effects** button.

- In the dialogue box displayed choose the required stretch and fill options. When finished click on **OK** in the dialogue box and apply the options by clicking **OK** in the **Format Data Series** dialogue box.

- To clear a graphic pasted on to a chart, select the column or data marker and choose **Clear** from the **Edit** menu and **Formats** from the sub-menu.

8.15 Regression Analysis

By establishing a trend, regression analysis enables you to forecast future values based on your existing data and display these on a chart. To create a trendline:

- Select the data series on which you wish to use a trendline.

- Choose **Add Trendline** from the **Chart** menu and a dialogue box will be presented. Select the **Type** tab and choose the type of trendline you require.

- If you wish to display the equation which was used to create the trendline Select the **Options** tab and click in the **Display Equation on Chart** box.

- Click on **OK** to display the trendline.

More sophisticated uses of trendlines are covered in the **Microsoft Excel Users' Guide**.

9.0 PRINTING CHARTS

Excel can either print charts embedded in a worksheet or just on their own.

To print a chart as part of a worksheet use the method of printing as in Section 6.

To print a chart only, ensure that it is either on a chart sheet or, if it is embedded, double-click on it to make it active. Print the chart using the same method as printing the worksheet.

By default charts printed on their own are printed in landscape orientation and to fill the page. To alter this choose **Page Setup** from the **File** menu.

The orientation can be altered from the **Page** tab. The area of the page that the chart fills can be altered from the **Chart** tab. If you wish to resize or position the chart in any other way click on the **Custom** button and on the **OK** button. The chart can then be resized by clicking and dragging the chart handles.

10.0 GRAPHICS

To add the finishing touches and personalise your worksheet or chart you can use Excel's Drawing Tools.

10.1

Adding Graphics to a Worksheet

- Click on the 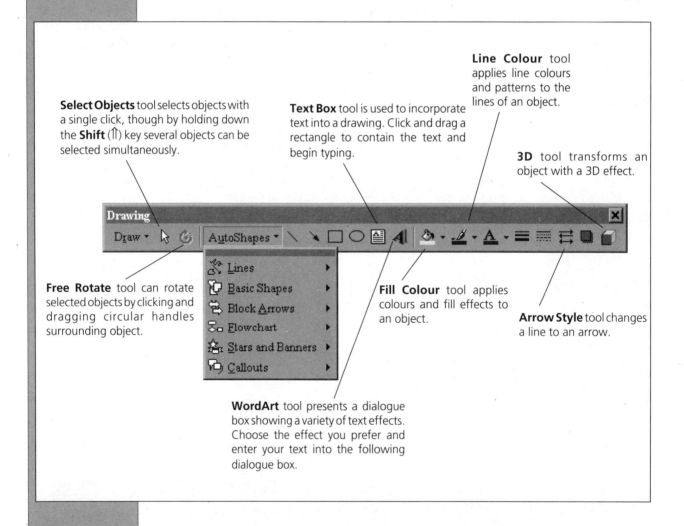 button on the toolbar.

- The **Drawing Toolbar** is displayed either as a standard Toolbar or as a floating Toolbar which can be dragged about the screen by its title bar.

10.2

Using the Drawing Tool to Draw Objects

Anything you draw using the tools is called an object. Several of the tools available from the Toolbar create geometric objects – the Rectangle, Oval, Line and Arrow tools create the most basic objects. To use these click on the preferred tool, move the pointer to the position on the window where you wish to start drawing, and click and drag until the object is the desired size. When you release the mouse button the object will be drawn.

Keep the **Shift** (⇧) key held down to draw objects symmetrically eg. a square or circle.

Other geometric objects, like block arrows, stars, flowchart symbols etc, are available from the **AutoShapes** pop-up menu on the **Drawing** toolbar.

Line Colour tool applies line colours and patterns to the lines of an object.

Select Objects tool selects objects with a single click, though by holding down the **Shift** (⇧) key several objects can be selected simultaneously.

Text Box tool is used to incorporate text into a drawing. Click and drag a rectangle to contain the text and begin typing.

3D tool transforms an object with a 3D effect.

Free Rotate tool can rotate selected objects by clicking and dragging circular handles surrounding object.

Lines
Basic Shapes
Block Arrows
Flowchart
Stars and Banners
Callouts

Fill Colour tool applies colours and fill effects to an object.

Arrow Style tool changes a line to an arrow.

WordArt tool presents a dialogue box showing a variety of text effects. Choose the effect you prefer and enter your text into the following dialogue box.

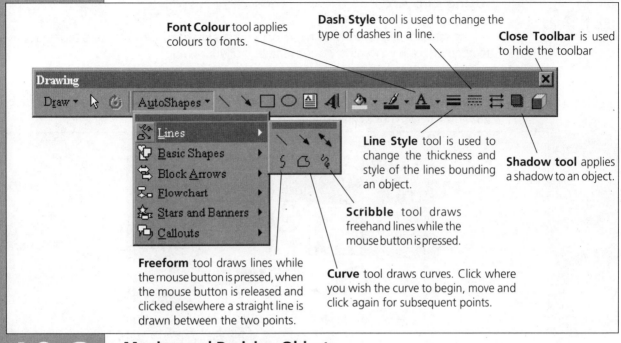

10.3 Moving and Resizing Objects

To move an object choose the **Select Objects** tool and click and drag on one of the lines of the object. When you release the mouse button the object will move to its new position.

To resize an object choose the **Select Objects** tool and click once on the object to display handles around its boundary. Click and drag on one of the handles to resize the object.

10.4 Deleting Objects

Select the object you wish to delete and press the **Backspace** (←) key.

10.5 The Draw Pop-up Menu

Commands available from the **Draw** pop-up menu enables you to manipulate one or more objects.

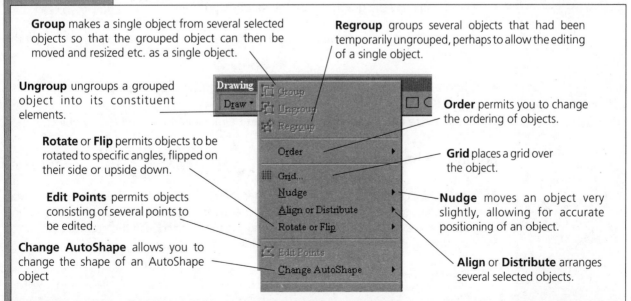

10.6 Using Clip Art

A large selection of pre-drawn artwork or Clip Art is provided with Excel and this can be used to good effect in enlivening the presentation of your work.

To use the Clip Art move the insertion point to where you wish the Clip Art to appear, choose **Picture** from the **Insert** menu and **Clip Art** from the sub-menu. From the dialogue box presented choose the required Clip Art.

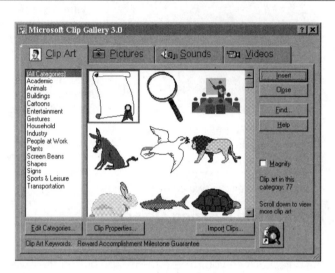

Clip Art can be moved and resized as any object. By default text around Clip Art is wrapped above and below the graphic.

10.7 Using Graphics Created by Another Program

While the graphics capabilities of Excel are sufficient for most uses there are times when only a dedicated graphics program will suffice. Fortunately once you have created your graphic it is a simple matter to insert it into your Excel worksheet and have it saved as part of the workbook.

- Select and copy the graphic from the graphics program.

- Open the Excel document and move the insertion point to where you wish to insert the graphic.

- Choose **Paste** from the **Edit** menu and the graphic will be inserted.

- Graphics created by another program can be moved and resized as any object.

10.8 Editing an Imported Graphic

To edit graphics created using a program other than Excel double-click on the graphic. This places a window around the graphic and Excel menus are replaced by those of the originating program. The graphic can now be edited using the tools provided in the program. Return to Excel by clicking outside the window surrounding the graphic.

11.0 EXCEL AS A DATABASE

A database is a store of information, systematically organised, which can be manipulated and retrieved by issuing instructions to the computer. For example, a database would allow you to sort a class list into alphabetical order and search for the name of a particular student. For most purposes like this which involve searching, sorting and extracting information from a simple list, Excel's database facility will prove adequate.

Terms defined:

There are some new terms used in connection with Excel's database which need to be understood:

Field – a column of the database.

Field Name – the name of the field entered into the first cell of the column.

Record – a row of the database.

11.1 Entering Data

Before you can use Excel as a database you must type your data into the cells as in the sample below ensuring that the first cell in each column is a field name.

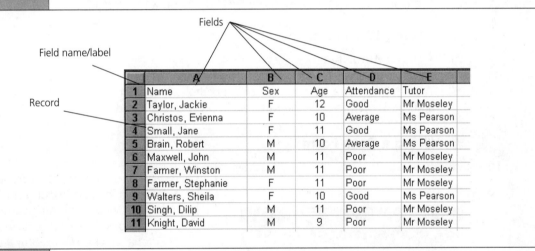

Fields

Field name/label

Record

	A	B	C	D	E
1	Name	Sex	Age	Attendance	Tutor
2	Taylor, Jackie	F	12	Good	Mr Moseley
3	Christos, Evienna	F	10	Average	Ms Pearson
4	Small, Jane	F	11	Good	Ms Pearson
5	Brain, Robert	M	10	Average	Ms Pearson
6	Maxwell, John	M	11	Poor	Mr Moseley
7	Farmer, Winston	M	11	Poor	Mr Moseley
8	Farmer, Stephanie	F	11	Poor	Mr Moseley
9	Walters, Sheila	F	10	Good	Ms Pearson
10	Singh, Dilip	M	11	Poor	Mr Moseley
11	Knight, David	M	9	Poor	Mr Moseley

11.2 Sorting Your Data

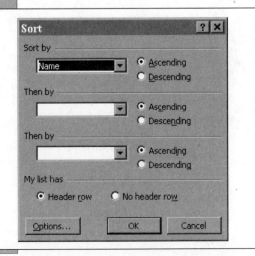

One of the most common manipulations is to sort records in a database. The sort can be numerical or alphabetic, and can be in ascending or descending order.

To sort your data:

- Select a single cell of the data to be sorted.

- Choose **Sort** from the **Data** menu.

The dialogue box opposite will be presented.

If the first row of data contains column labels Excel uses these to sort the data. By default this starts with the first label of the row. Sorting our sample data in this way would result in the rows being re-ordered alphabetically based upon the name of the student. To sort the data using a different column label, for example, Age, click on the arrow alongside the **Sort By** section of the dialogue box and choose Age.

If you wish you may sort using more than one column label, eg. to sort our sample into Tutor and Age. Set up **Sort By** as Tutor, and set up a **Then By** as Age.

To change the order of the sort click on the **Ascending** or **Descending** buttons.

If you wish to sort only a portion of your data, select just this data and follow the procedure above.

Buttons on the Toolbar provide a short cut to sorting. Use the ⬛ button to sort a list into ascending order and the ⬛ button to sort into descending order.

12.0 MANIPULATING A DATABASE

Excel allows you to filter your data so that only data conforming to certain criteria is displayed.

There are two main ways of using Excel to filter data:

- Using a **Data Form**. See Section 12.1.

- Using **AutoFilter**. See Section 12.4.

Though Excel has a filtering method for complex criteria, it is beyond the scope of this guide and you should refer to the **Microsoft Excel Users' Guide**.

12.1 Using a Data Form

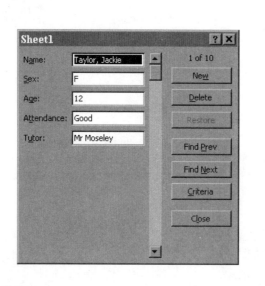

A Data Form is the easiest method of searching a database for a particular record. It cannot, however, be used to examine several records simultaneously or extract data based on a set of criteria. To use a Data Form select a single cell of the data to be filtered and choose **Form** from the **Data** menu. A dialogue box like the one opposite is presented though its exact appearance will vary according to the nature of your own data.

The dialogue box shows the details of a single record. Field names for each record are presented on the left of the dialogue box; alongside each field name is a box displaying data from each field. Initially this will contain the data from the first record to move to other records use the scroll bar.

12.2

Adding, Deleting and Amending Records

To add a record, click on the **New** button and enter the data for your new record in the blank boxes alongside the field names.

To delete a record, use the scroll bar to display the record you wish to delete and click on the **Delete** button. A dialogue box will be displayed asking for confirmation and warning you that the record will be deleted permanently from the worksheet.

To amend a record, use the scroll bar to display the record you wish to change. Make the changes by altering the contents of the boxes alongside the field names. To revert to the original entry click on the **Restore** button.

12.3

Searching Using a Data Form

To search using a Data Form it is necessary to have some basis for your search – the criteria. To input your search criteria click on the **Criteria** button. This will display a dialogue box listing the field names with boxes alongside for entry of the criteria.

The criteria entered in the boxes depends upon the purpose and nature of your search. To search for a record containing a particular field entry, type in the appropriate box alongside the field name and click on the **Find Next** button. If a record containing the entry is present in the database it will be displayed in the data form; if more than one record conforms to the criteria by clicking again on the **Find Next** button other records will be displayed. If no record complies with the criteria a warning note is sounded.

The following operators can also be used if the field entry is numerical:

=	Equal to	>=	Greater than or equal to
>	Greater than	<=	Less than of equal to
<	Less than	<>	Not equal to

By entering one of the above operators followed by a number into the field entry box the criteria can be specified further. For example, with our sample data, if >10 was entered into the age field entry box, when the **Find Next** button is clicked only records of students older than 10 will be displayed in the Data Form.

More than one field entry box can be used to specify criteria for each search.

11.4

Using AutoFilter

Using the Data Form to search your database is often perfectly adequate but if you wish to examine several records simultaneously or extract data based on a set of criteria, then you need to use the AutoFilter method.

	A	B	C	D	E	F
1	Name	Sex	Age	Attendanc	Tutor	
2	Taylor, Jackie	F	[All]	Good	Mr Moseley	
3	Christos, Evienna	F	[Top 10...]	Average	Ms Pearson	
4	Small, Jane	F	[Custom...]	Good	Ms Pearson	
5	Brain, Robert	M	9	Average	Ms Pearson	
6	Maxwell, John	M	10	Poor	Mr Moseley	
7	Farmer, Winston	M	11	Poor	Mr Moseley	
8	Farmer, Stephanie	F	11	Poor	Mr Moseley	
9	Walters, Sheila	F	10	Good	Ms Pearson	
10	Singh, Dilip	M	11	Poor	Mr Moseley	
11	Knight, David	M	9	Poor	Mr Moseley	
12						
13						
14						

Select a single cell of the data to be filtered. Choose **Filter** from the **Data** menu and **AutoFilter** from the sub-menu. This will cause drop-down arrows to be displayed alongside the column labels. Clicking on one of these arrows will display a list of all unique items in the column, and by selecting one of these you choose to display only those records which conform to this criterion.

The list can be filtered further by choosing other criteria from different columns.

- To remove a filter from a column use the drop-down arrow to choose **(All)**.

- To remove all filters choose **Filter** from the **Data** menu and **Show All** from the sub-menu.

- To turn off AutoFilter choose **Filter** from the **Data** menu and **AutoFilter** from the sub-menu.

Using Custom Criteria with AutoFilter

Often you will want to filter more complex criteria than these listed directly under the drop-down arrows. For example, using our sample data you might wish to find all those students who are older than 11.

To enter custom criteria choose **Custom** from the drop-down arrow, and the dialogue box below will be displayed.

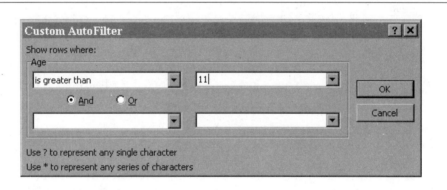

Enter the required criterion, if necessary, using the operators available from the pop-up menus in the dialogue box. The dialogue box displayed shows the criteria to select all students older than 11.

Using AND Criteria

The above example uses only a single criterion. However, sometimes it is necessary to specify more than one criterion, eg. if you wish to filter only the data for students that are female AND aged above 11. This kind of filter is called an **AND** filter because the data is filtered only if it conforms to one criterion AND another.

To filter the sample data according to the criteria above using AND, enter **F** as criteria under the Sex column label and **Custom** under the Age column label. Enter **is greater than** and **11** as the custom criterion.

Alternatively you might wish to filter only the data for students older than 10 AND younger than 11. To filter the sample data according to these criteria, choose **Custom** under the Age column label. Enter **is greater than** and **10** into the upper section of the dialogue box and **is less than** and **11** into the lower section. Ensure the **And** button is selected and click on **OK** to filter the data.

12.7 Using OR Criteria

OR is useful if you wish to filter data based on one set of criteria OR another, eg. if you wish to filter only the data for students older than 11 OR younger than 10.

To filter the sample data according to the criteria above using OR, choose **Custom** under the Age column label. Enter **is less than** and **10** into the upper section of the dialogue box and **is greater than** and **11** into the lower section. Click on the **Or** button and on **OK** to filter the data.

12.8 Text as Part of the Custom Criteria

Text typed into the custom criteria can be used to filter data if either the data matches the criteria exactly or the first few characters (letters or numbers) match the data.

> **Note**: Custom text criteria are case sensitive.

If you wish to filter data based upon an exact match with text in the criteria then just enter the text into the custom criteria dialogue box and click on **OK**.

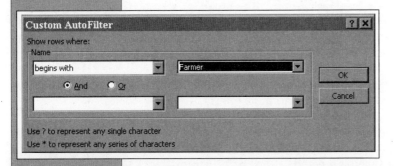

To filter data based upon the first text contained in the cell enter **begins with** and the text as the criterion, our sample opposite will filter all Names beginning with **Farmer**.

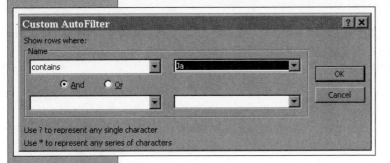

To filter data based upon any text contained in the cell enter **contains** and the text as the criterion, our sample opposite will filter all Names containing **Ja**.

12.9 Extracting Filtered Data

Data which has been filtered using the AutoFilter method above can be extracted from the database by using copy and paste.

To do this select the filtered data and choose **Copy** from the **Edit** menu. Move the insertion point to where you wish to copy the data and choose **Paste** from the **Edit** menu.

> **Note**: You may paste filtered data to another part of the worksheet, another worksheet, another workbook, or even to a document created by a different program.

APPENDIX A

APPENDIX A

ERROR MESSAGES

If a formula is incorrect in any way Excel will display an error message in the cell into which the formula is typed. The error messages and their meanings are as follows:

This means that the column containing the number is not wide enough to display its contents. See Section 2.12 on how to increase the width of a column.

#DIV/0!   This means that the formula is trying to divide by zero. The most likely cause is that you have referenced a blank cell or a cell containing zero.

#N/A   This means that no value is available for one of the cells that you have referenced.

#NAME?   This means you have used a formula name that Excel does not recognise. Maybe you mis-spelled it or forgot to put a colon in between cell references.

#NUM!   This means there is a problem with a number. Maybe you have used an unacceptable argument with a formula or you have produced a number using a formula which is too large or small to be represented by Excel.

#REF!   This means that you have referred to a cell that is not valid. Maybe you have deleted a cell to which a formula refers.

#VALUE!   This means you have used the wrong type of argument. Maybe you have not put the = sign before the formula or you have typed text into a formula where numbers were expected.

APPENDIX B

FUNCTIONS

There are a great many Functions built in to Excel. However, you will use only a handful of these on a regular basis and so only the most commonly used functions are listed below with a brief explanation. For information regarding other functions refer to the Excel Help facility.

Financial Functions

ACCRINT	Accrued interest for security paying periodic interest.
ACCRINTM	Accrued interest for security paying interest at maturity.
CUMIPMT	Cumulative interest paid between two periods.
CUMPRINC	Cumulative principal paid on loan between two periods.
DB	Depreciating asset for specified period fixed-declining balance.
DDB	Depreciating asset for specified period double-declining balance.
DISC	Discount rate for security.
DURATION	Duration of security with periodic interest payments.
EFFECT	Effective annual interest rate.
FV	Future value of investment.
FVSCHEDULE	Future value of principal after series of cumulative period interest rates.
INTRATE	interest rate for fully invested security.
IPMT	interest payment for an investment for given period.
MIRR	Internal rate of return where positive and negative cash flows are financed at different rates.
NOMINAL	Annual nominal interest rate.
NPER	Number periods for an investment.
NPV	Net present value of investment based on series of periodic cash flows and discount rate.
PMT	Periodic payment for an annuity.
PPMT	Payment on principal for an investment for period.
PV	Present value of an investment.
RATE	Interest rate /period of annuity.
RECEIVED	Amount received at maturity for fully invested security.
SLN	Straight-line depreciating of asset for one period.
SYD	Sum-of-years digits depreciating of asset for specific period.
YIELD	Yield on security paying periodic interest.
YIELDDISC	Annual yield for discounted security.
YIELDMAT	Annual yield of security paying interest at maturity.

Mathematical & Trigonometric Functions

ABS	Absolute value of number.
ACOS	Arccosine of number.
ASIN	Arcsine of number.
ATAN	Arctangent of number.
ATAN2	Arctangent from x-and y-coordinates.
BASE	Converts base -10 number into another base.
CEILING	Rounds number up to the nearest integer.
COMBIN	Number combinations for given number objects.
COS	Cosine of number.
EVEN	Rounds number up to the nearest even integer.
EXP	e raised to the power of given number.
FACT	Factorial of number.
FLOOR	Rounds number down, toward zero.

APPENDIX B

GCD	Greatest common divisor.
INT	Rounds number down to the nearest integer.
LCM	Least common multiple.
LN	Natural logarithm of number.
LOG	Logarithm of number to specified base.
LOG10	Base-10 logarithm of number.
MOD	Remainder from division.
MROUND	Number rounded to the desired multiple.
ODD	Rounds number up to the nearest odd integer.
PI	Value Pi.
PRODUCT	Multiplies its arguments.
QUOTIENT	Integer part of division.
RAND	Random number between 0 and 1.
RANDBET	Random number between the numbers you specify.
ROUND	Rounds number to specified number digits.
SIGN	Sign of number.
SIN	Sine of the given angle.
SQRT	Positive square root.
SQRTPI	Square root of number.
SUM	Adds its arguments.
SUMSQ	Sum of squares of the arguments.
TAN	Tangent of number.
TRUNC	Truncates number to an integer.

Statistical Functions

AVEDEV	Average of the absolute deviation of data points from their mean.
AVERAGE	Average of its arguments.
BINOMDIST	Individual term binomial distribution.
CHIDIST	1-tailed probability of the chi squared distribution.
CHIINV	Inverse of the chi-squared distribution.
CHITEST	Test for independence.
CONFIDENCE	Confidence interval for population.
CORREL	Correlation coefficient between two data sets.
COUNT	Counts how many numbers are in the list of arguments.
COUNTA	Counts how many values are in the list of arguments.
COVAR	Covariance, the ave. of the products of paired deviations.
CRITBINOM	Smallest value for which the cumulative binomial distribution is less than or equal to criterion value.
DEVSQ	Sum of squares of deviations.
EXPONDIST	Exponential distribution.
FDIST	F probability distribution.
FINV	Inverse of the F probability distribution.
FISHER	Fisher transformation.
FISHERINV	Inverse of the Fisher transformation.
FORECAST	value along linear trend.
FTEST	Result of an F-test.
GEOMEAN	Geometric mean.
GROWTH	Values along an exponential trend.
HARMEAN	Harmonic mean.
INTERCEPT	Intercept of the linear regression line.
KURT	Kurtosis of data set.
LARGE	K-th largest value in data set.
LINEST	Parameters of linear trend.
LOGEST	Parameters of an exponential trend.
LOGINV	Inverse of the lognormal distribution.

APPENDIX B

LOGNORMDIST	Lognormal distribution.
MAX	Maximum value in list of arguments.
MEDIAN	Median of the given numbers.
MIN	Minimum value in list of arguments.
MODE	Most common value in data set.
NORMDIST	Normal cumulative distribution.
NORMSDIST	Standard normal cumulative distribution.
PEARSON	Pearson product moment correlation coefficient.
PERCENTILE	K-th percentile of values in range.
PERCENTRANK	Percentage rank of value in data set.
POISSON	Poisson probability distribution.
PROB	Probability that values in range are between two limits.
RANK	Rank of number in list of numbers.
RSQ	R^2 value of the linear regression line.
SKEW	Skewness of distribution.
SLOPE	Slope of the linear regression line.
SMALL	K-th smallest value in data set.
STDEV	Estimates standard deviation based on sample.
STDEVP	Calculates standard deviation based on the entire Population.
STEYX	Standard error of predicted y-value for each x the regression.
TDIST	Student's t-distribution.
TINV	Inverse of the Student's t-distribution.
TREND	Values along linear trend.
TTEST	Probability associated with a Student's t-Test.
VAR	Estimates variance based on sample.
VARP	Calculates variance based on the entire population.
ZTEST	Two-tailed P-value of z-test.

Logical Functions

AND	TRUE if all its arguments are TRUE.
FALSE	Logical value FALSE.
IF	Specifies logical test to perform.
NOT	Reverses the logic of its argument.
OR	TRUE if any argument is TRUE.
TRUE	Logical value TRUE.

Statistical Macro Functions

ANOVA1	Single-factor analysis of variance.
ANOVA2	Two-factor analysis of variance with replication.
ANOVA3	Two-factor analysis of variance without replication.
DESCR	Descriptive statistics for data in the input range.
FTESTV	Two-sample F-test.
MCOVAR	Covariance between two or more data sets.
PTTESTM	Paired Two-sample Student's t-Test for means.
PTTESTV	Two-sample Student's t-Test, unequal variances.
REGRESS	Multiple linear regression analysis.
TTESTM	Two-sample Student's t-Test for means, equal variances.
ZTESTM	Two-sample z-test for means, variances.

APPENDIX C

Importing and Exporting Data

Moving data to and from other programs is extremely useful since it allows you to mix the capabilities of Excel with the specialist features of other programs such as graphics or wordprocessing programs. It also avoids both the labour of re-typing and the possibility of introducing errors.

Note: In this Appendix Windows 3, 3.1 and 3.11 are collectively referred to as Windows.

Importing Data

There are two ways of importing data from other programs into Excel.

- By cutting and pasting data into Excel.

- By saving the data in a format that can be opened by Excel.

Cutting and Pasting Data into Excel from other Windows 95 programs

The way that you Cut, Copy and Paste between programs is more or less the same. Here is an example of how to copy data from almost any program into Excel.

Select the data in the program. Choose **Copy** from the **Edit** Menu. **Exit** the program. Open Excel. Select the place where you wish the data to appear, and choose **Paste** from the **Edit** menu.

Note: Some programs, eg. Word and Access, allow pasted data to be edited within Excel. Double-clicking on the pasted data changes the menu bar to that of the originating program allowing the data to be edited. Click outside the area of the data to revert to Excel's menu bar.

Importing Saved Data

Importing data already saved has the advantage that you have a stored copy should anything go wrong. It is also the easiest way to transfer data between different types of computer, eg. Windows PC or Macintosh to Windows 95 PC.

Data from another program needs to have been saved in a format that Excel can understand. However in most cases you will find that Excel can open files without any need to resort to saving in a different file format.

Excel 97 can import the following file formats: Text (space and tab delimited), CSV, SYLK, WKS, Lotus 1-2-3 (WK1-4), Quattro Pro (WQ1), DIF, DBF2-4, Excel 2-5, Excel 95/7. In most cases you will import data in "Text" form unless you are importing a file from another spreadsheet program.

The method used to import any kind of saved data is into Excel is more or less the same.

- **Exit** the program and open Excel.

- Select **Open** from the **File** menu. This will present a dialogue box. Click on the arrow to **List Files of Type** and choose **All Files**. Select the file you wish to import and click on **Open**. The file will be converted into Excel 97 for Windows 95 format.

Note: When opening files containing formulae from other Spreadsheet programs Excel will attempt to convert formulae, but in some cases this will not be possible and an error message will result.

APPENDIX C

Importing Data from a Windows Program

The method used is as above except that the file must be saved onto a floppy disc before it can be imported.

Importing Data from a Macintosh Program

Most data saved on a Macintosh can be imported into Excel 97. The basic procedure is the same as above except that the disc used to save the file on must be in PC disk format and filenames should contain no more than 8 characters. The Apple File Exchange or PC Exchange programs supplied with every Macintosh can be used to create the PC formatted disc. Save the file on the disc and open it using Excel, as described above.

Exporting Data

There are two ways of exporting data to another program from Excel.

- By copying and pasting data.

- By using saved data.

Using Copy and Paste

This method will only work for exporting to other Windows 95 programs.

Select the data you wish to export and Copy it. Close Excel. Open the program to which you wish to export the data. Move the insertion point to where you wish the data to appear and choose **Paste** from the **Edit** menu.

> **Note**: unless pasting to another spreadsheet only the results or values of any calculations are pasted from Excel, not the formulae that went to create them.

If copying from Word ensure that the data for each column is separated (delimited) by tabs or in table format before selecting.

Using Saved Data

This is the only way to export data to some Windows 95 programs and all Windows and Macintosh programs.

Open the data you wish to export. Choose **Save As** from the **File** menu. Click on the arrow alongside the **Save File As Type** box and select the file type that you know can be imported by your program (see file types above). Open the file as normal.

> **Remember**: not all formats save all the information contained in an Excel 97 file. For example, Text or CSV will not save any formatting. So make sure that you keep a copy of the workbook in normal Excel 97 format.

> **Note**: If you wish to export data to Excel 5.0, or Excel 95/7 for Windows 95 save your data in the file format Microsoft Excel 97 & 5.0/workbook.

Exporting Data to a Windows Program

The basic procedure is the same as above except that before the files can be opened they must be renamed so that they conform to the usual 8 character filenames of Windows.

Exporting Data to a Macintosh Program

The basic procedure is the same as above except that the filename should consist of no more than 8 characters and before the files can be opened they must be transferred to the Macintosh using the Apple File Exchange or PC Exchange programs supplied with every Macintosh. Once transferred the file can be opened from the Macintosh program as normal.

Notes...

Notes...